GRIEF
IS A
GATEWAY

GRIEF

IS A

GATEWAY

Encountering God
Through Seasons of Loss

GUERLYNE GUERCY

ISBN 979-8-9931760-2-4 (Paperback)
ISBN 979-8-9931760-3-1 (E-book)
ISBN 979-8-9931760-4-8 (PDF)

Library of Congress Control Number: 2025921119

Printed in the United States of America.

This book is dedicated to my Lord and Savior Jesus Christ, my Constant, my Comforter.

The One who first loved me and embraced me wholly when my heart was in fragments and continually shows me abundant grace.

The One who gave me an inescapable burden for this work and orchestrated the circumstances for it to be completed in the fullness of His time.

Here it is, Lord.

May You be glorified and honored above all.

Acknowledgments

A heartfelt thanks to:

My adoring parents, Jacques & Guetelyne, who, through their unwavering love and support, have paved the runway for me to pursue my dreams.

My amazing family who have walked alongside me in season and for their constant love and support.

My wonderful friends who have witnessed the journey to these pages and encouraged me beyond my own limitations into purpose.

My brilliant editor, Jazmine, who helped me find the truest form of my voice and guided my words with the utmost grace.

Contents

Introduction

G rief is one of the most unique, bewildering, tender, and personal parts of the human experience. It does not wear a single face. It arrives in moments we expect and in moments we never saw coming. It can be loud and overwhelming or quiet and lingering. Sometimes, it feels like an ache we can name. Other times, it hides behind the loss of what was or what could've been.

Loss is not relegated to just death; it can stem from the end of a dream, a relationship at the end of its road, or the subtle unraveling of who we thought we'd be by now. It is found in seasons of transition and moments of disappointment– when God's delay feels like a denial.

This book is for those kinds of grief.

However, here, we're not focusing solely on the primary losses– though those are sacred too– but rather, the often-unspoken, intangible voids. The moments we rarely grieve out loud. The ones that linger in our spirits and affect how we see ourselves, our faith, and even our God. These moments might go unnamed by others, but they are not unnoticed by the One who formed us.

Grief Is a Gateway is not intended to give quick answers or spiritual cliches. Instead, this book serves as an invitation, much like how loss extends itself, because grief is more than pain: it is a gateway– a sacred point of entry where a divine encounter awaits. The coming chapters will serve as a guided reflection with the intention to excavate and uncover potential overlooked losses, with hopes of acknowledging the loss as a catalyst to the path to encounter God more in depth by allowing Him to walk with us in our valley and lift our eyes and hearts from that place of despair. And while the path through it may be winding and hard, it can also lead us to the heart of God's comfort. Scripture reminds us in Psalm 34:18, "The Lord is near to the brokenhearted and saves the crushed in spirit." This nearness is not just symbolic—it's *real*. And it changes everything.

We don't have to come out of this season the same way we entered it. With Christ, what feels like ruin can become restoration. What feels like a void can be filled with His presence, peace, and power. It's a turning point in our faith. A sacred pause to sit in what's been lost... and open our hearts to what might be gained.

In the pages that follow, we'll walk together through scripture, personal stories, and spiritual reflection to discover that grief is not the end. It's a beginning– a holy invitation to meet the Comforter in the space where only He can go.

So I ask you, gently and sincerely: Are you ready to enter through the sacred gateway of grief?

Let us pray:

Heavenly Father,

*I pray for this reader on the other side of
this book and ask that in these pages You would minister
to them in a way that only You can.*

*Beyond the words You've inspired through me, I pray
your child comes to know You in the fullness of Your
perfect grace through the blood of Your Son, Jesus Christ,
who died and rose again for their sins so that they may
experience You in their season of grief in an
undeniable way.*

*Cause Your scriptures come alive for them as you renew
their hope in You to the point of rest.*

*I thank You and praise You Lord for the healing that
awaits them in your comforting arms as they pass through
the gateway of grief.*

*In Jesus' Name,
Amen.*

Chapter 1

Loss: A Shaking and a Shaping

1

Loss: A Shaking and a Shaping

In life, there are many losses we incur, and assuredly, just as we live, we will also experience loss as part of our human experience. Generally, when we hear the term 'loss,' we most closely associate that with a loved one; however, we can experience loss in many other areas of our life. A "loss" is the state or feeling of grief when *deprived* of someone or something of value. For that reason, loss can be subjective, and subsequently, grief is then our response to the *loss* of what we value. It is our natural emotional response to the sudden absence of what we have deemed important or significant.

Typically, we associate that with our loved ones, but we can all attest to the many losses we have experienced in our lives beyond loved ones, which are often left discounted, and some of which can be seemingly back to back; it is often these areas that fester untended and eventually overtake us at inopportune times.

As believers in Christ, we have a hope and assurance in Him, which is why although death may have its finality, we have an eternal hope in Christ Jesus beyond the grave.

Our response to loss is often a mirror of where we are in our spiritual journey whenever that loss occurs. Likewise, we can pinpoint when we have felt the most poignant loss, or grief exposure in our life. Fortunately for us, grief is a unique and tailored attention-getter that will expose our theology (what we really believe about God). First, we need to identify and acknowledge our loss.

Most frequently, we think immediately about a *primary* loss like a person or loved one, and often forget about the myriad of *secondary losses or intangible* ones we experience in the course of life which are often difficult and unrecognized areas.[1] It is indeed possible to lose and thereafter need to grieve intangible things as well, such as but not limited to:

- Relationships
- Roles
- Divorce
- Friendships
- Fertility
- Dreams
- Opportunities

- Potential
- Personal Identity
- Employment
- Bodily Functions
- Illnesses
- Other life transitions

No matter what comes to mind while reading these pages or even reflecting on how you've already experienced a combination of the two, we can agree it *stung*. While or whether experiencing these losses, they can be sudden, violent, or even progressive.

The Bible says "better is the end of a thing than the beginning thereof, and the patient in spirit is better than the proud in spirit" (Ecc. 7:8). We also know Ecclesiastes chapter 3– pronounced at every funeral or homegoing service to our chagrin– lists the variety or range of seasons and emotions we experience in this life.

"To every thing there is a season, and a time to every purpose under thc heaven..."

This means life is characterized by the seasonality of it; like nature, we have winter, spring, summer, and fall. He then goes on to list seven lines of reference, but for sake of discussion let's look at verses 4 and 6: "...a time to weep, and a time to laugh; a time to mourn, and a time to dance; A time to get, and a time to lose; a time to keep, and a time to cast away..." Both these verses speak to primary and secondary losses. Although each counter to the experience is almost hard to perceive experiencing, that speaks of balance in life.

To every thing there is a season, and a time to every purpose under the heaven...

Ecclesiastes 3:1

We have positives and negatives, much like a battery, which cancels each other out to be effective. For instance, when we are overwhelmed in mourning, it's hard to conceive one day we will laugh again, and just as we will gain, we will also lose. This chapter is preparing us for the eventuality that befalls us all.

No matter which seasons we are in, friend, it is still a *shock* when the season changes, even when we know to expect it. Depending on the location, if we experience winter seasons, we know winter is coming, and yet when we walk into the briskness of the air, the shock of the temperature is still unpleasant.

As someone raised in New York, I will never get used to cold weather. I may understand that "it's that time of year" for my Northface jacket and boots, but that doesn't make it any more pleasurable to experience because I inherently don't enjoy cold weather. And likewise, the variety of season of loss we find ourselves in right

now may deliver a shock of sorts
to our faith which we could liken
to the temperature. Someone may
say, "just move to a warmer climate
if you don't like that weather," but
we see how global warming has us
all experiencing unusual tempera-
tures in regions we never thought

**We have to be sure our
foundation is in Christ
and we stand on His
word for our lives.**

we would. Unfortunately, neither you nor I are exempt from that
shock, regardless what location we traverse to, as it is in our walk
with Christ: loss is unavoidable.

Loss has a unique property laced within it to make us question
God's intention and ask why or question everything. Who, what,
where, when, why *and* how! I'm sure many of us have thought to
ourselves:

"I loved this person, why must they die now?"

"I love this job, I make great money, why did I lose it?"

"What did I do wrong?"

"If I only said [this] then they'd still be here?"

"I thought I knew who I was, but who am I now?"

As many questions as we have for God in the midst of our loss,
the experience now dispenses the same to us concerning our faith.
It's like a compound car crash scene because our faith is now tested
on every side in ways we may have not, otherwise, encountered
(2 Cor. 4:8-9).

Now ask yourself, in the face of the absence of [insert the person
or thing], now who is God to me? Or the one I asked indignantly,
"What kind of God would take _____ from me?!" Herein lies the
crisis of faith and theology (the study of the nature of God and reli-

gious belief) because depending on how attached we were to said person or thing, our belief system is now in conflict with the character of God that has chosen to take *that* and challenge if we *really* believe God is God. We wonder, "how could this be the nature of the God I serve?" It is seldom out of curiosity that we pose this question as much as it is an accusation and prideful challenge to the omniscience of the perfect all-knowing God we claim to serve.

Let's look at the parable of the wise and foolish builders in Matthew 7:25-27 NIV:

> The rain came down, the streams rose, and the
> winds blew and beat against that house; yet it did not
> fall, because it had its foundation on the rock.
> But everyone who hears these words of mine and does
> not put them into practice is like a foolish man who
> built his house on sand. The rain came down, the
> streams rose, and the winds blew and beat against that
> house, and it fell with a great crash.

In this particular text, Jesus illustrates a powerful message by comparing a house built by a notably wise man on rock, compared to the foolish man who built his on sand and could not withstand the storm that came. Similarly, we will experience storms of loss in many directions. The assurance in these verses and this example here is that one, a storm will come, and two, the foundation will be challenged. So friend, we cannot not let our grief cause us to fall with a great crash (v.27) and overtake us. We have to be sure our foundation is in Christ and we stand on His word for our lives.

In our walk *with* Christ, our foundation must start with Christ. Much like the first step in building a home, a foundation in Jesus is the first step. Losses will come; they can be in a wind and swift or in a stream of loss, gradually rising as we see in the text.

However, one thing is certain: how our foundation is laid will make room for how we respond to that loss. As the wise man in verse 25, the house was "beat against...yet it did not fall." This tells us that our losses will certainly challenge us, and despite that challenge, we can still stand.

I've experienced a combination of primary and intangible losses, from family members passing away in consecutive years, jobs, identity, and one of my faculties temporarily lost before being restored again. Each loss found me in a different season and called for different lessons, but I would be remiss not to acknowledge how my initial take left me very dissatisfied and disappointed with how I thought God responded to me. In hindsight, on this side of grief, I can now say His character has been consistent and gave me cause to love him the more, which is from where this admonishment and lessons come– we press into that shock, contend with God, and praise Him all the more.

Key Points:

- We can experience grief in many intangible or ambiguous areas beyond primary loss (of people).

- Loss will expose our theology.

- In our walk with Christ, our foundation must start *with* Christ (Matt. 7:25-27).

Reflection & Exercise:

1. Acknowledge your loss: Who or what did you lose? List the areas you have previously or are currently experiencing loss.

2. What was the first loss you experienced? Was it in your childhood or adulthood? Looking at your list, which loss is the most fresh to you?

3. Ask yourself: Am I ready to grieve my loss? Am I grieving my loss now? Or have I not begun processing my loss?

4. How has that loss affected your walk with Christ?

5. Read Ecclesiastes 3:1-8. What "time" or season is this for you?

Notes

Chapter 2

A Hardened Heart

2

A Hardened Heart

Natural disasters can befall us in many different forms: hurricanes, tornados, earthquakes, floods, etc. For those directly impacted or in the eye of the disaster, we sometimes have time to stock up and prepare, whereas in other instances there's no time to prepare, and it forces us into evacuation or displacement. For example, with earthquakes, scientists describe them as an intense shaking of the earth's surface caused by movements in the outermost layer, which causes pieces of the earth's crust to bump into or slide against one another. In some earthquakes, people experience what feels like a truck coming too close to their car and the vibrations of it shake it, barely making a wave. Whereas stronger earthquakes can destroy homes, ruin roadways, and cause rockslides in certain areas. In a nutshell, it can cause destruction. Then there's the aftershock-- tremors that transpire after the initial earthquake. A reverberation of that first wave seismic activity.

The basis of comparison when it comes to earthquakes and grief is that they both are unpredictable. They shake foundations and reverberate throughout our lives. The tectonic plates below us shift to seismic proportions, and the Richter scale of our faith is off the charts before we know it. That moment is one of the most crucial because we make a subconscious decision to either be angry with God or to create an outlet to process the blow. The Bible tells us in Ephesians 4:26, "Be ye angry, and sin not: let not the sun go down upon your wrath," meaning that anger is a natural emotion to have, but it is not license to sin. When our hearts are broken because the injury from the loss is great, we just as easily can turn the anger inward towards ourselves.

How disappointment festers

One of the insidious aspects about secondary losses is they are intangible in a way we almost don't know where to direct our frustration. Disappointments and unmet expectations that have nowhere to go somehow find themselves lodged in our own hearts. That thinking is where the enemy loves to widen the chasm between us and God by depositing these kinds of thoughts.

As we learned, grief is often a mirror of our theology, what we believe of God to be true, and where we are in our walk with Christ. When these losses transpire, that same mirror of our theology will now challenge the true attributes of God and what we've since ascribed to God.

For instance, I remember a season when I was disappointed with the course of my career, not getting promotions and recognition, not fully understanding I was in a season of transition but was still easily triggered to indulge in alcohol when I felt hopeless (that was how I processed my despair). I remember the Lord whispering to me Psalm 61:2: "From the end of the earth will I cry unto thee, when my heart is overwhelmed: lead me to the rock that is higher than I.”

The B clause is what really ministered to me in that moment because in my overwhelm and the onslaught of disappointment that swelled over me, God's voice arrested me in that moment to seek Him before I sought what I thought my flesh would need through the use of alcohol. I knew it was God working because typically, I'd already have my keys in hand on the way to my nearest liquor store. Instead, my first inclination was to go to God first. That split moment in overwhelm is

That split moment in overwhelm is where we can either choose our pain or the whisper of His voice.

where we can either choose our pain or the whisper of His voice. His whisper overrode that painful instance, not because it was louder in decimals, but because my need for the rock that is higher than I was greater than temporary satisfaction.

Faith is paradoxical in that way; it necessitates we draw nigh to Him (James 4:18) which is contrary to our nature and try to “fill” or assuage our overwhelm with the temporary void-filler of choice. That is precisely when we should draw near to Him because when we do not, we encroach upon the territory where we take counsel in our own heart, which we know is deceitful and desperately wicked (Jeremiah 17:9) while simultaneously hardening it.

We may be angry and the multitude of emotions may, too, be great, but this is precisely where that overwhelm and onslaught of emotion will meet a very willing Savior. If we're keeping it real, it is also in those moments when we have to go outside ourselves and see we're not even really mad at that person for leaving the relationship, abandoning the friendship, betraying our trust, or the company for firing us as much as we are at the God who *allowed* the devastation that left our heart in overwhelm and disrepair.

The ache of disappointment and loss has a way of piercing our heart in a way that is so unique to the particular loss.

It is in moments like those where Proverbs 13:12 comes to mind that tells us, "Hope *deferred* makes the heart sick, but a longing fulfilled is a tree of life." Hopelessness or absence of hope is typically the direct feeling to describe that ache. When something is deferred, it is put off for a later time, yet when what we want evades us for reasons beyond our control, it then causes us to grow in resentment towards God, thus "...making the heart sick" (v.12). The gap between what we desire and reality is where hope waivers and the questions ensue. For example, how will I go on now that this person is gone? How will I recover from this financial impact? Will I ever be happy again? It's like we cannot see this longing fulfilled in that present moment.

The A clause in the above mentioned scripture refers to sickness because we can literally have a visceral physical reaction to the point we don't want to eat, drink, laugh, or continue with life's daily moments. When we are physically sick, or have a virus of sorts, it changes our normal routines and can spread to other parts of our bodies while simultaneously fighting for a semblance of normalcy or until our white blood cells kick in. That level of despair easily makes us sick *progressively* and therefore makes our immune resistance low.

Some losses are progressive in nature while others are more sudden. Neither are pleasurable, but they are equally losses worthy of vigilance. Similarly, our spiritual system is penetrated and injured and left open to being susceptible to other forms of sickness such as bitterness and anger, and before we know it, a full fledged hardened heart.

Then that hardened heart can turn into a backsliding state where we are out of God's will and are turned over to a reprobate mind (Romans 1:28).

These forms of sickness are not often kindled overnight; these usually develop after a cacophonic culmination of losses that we do not process.

My aunt (Tati) Vivie's passing

My earthquake moment in my adulthood was in my early twenties when my Tati Vivie passed away of stomach cancer. (In Haitian culture, the Creole equivalent for Aunt is *Tati* or *Tootz*, as I affectionately called her.) When this seismic event happened, I had backslid in my faith, and frankly, I was angry with God. Her death holds so much significance, not just for our relationship, but because of the immense impact it had on my spiritual journey and how it shook my faith.

My aunt was a woman of faith. In her later years, she gave her life to Christ and devoted her life and time to being a youth minister to young women, led praise dance ministry, as well as did administrative duties for her local church.

Tatie Vivie lived in Florida and we in New York, so we took multiple 24-hour long road trips down I-95. As her condition continued to worsen, it felt as though we would return home all to turn back again. Cancer is such a precarious condition and a complicated grieving process because we tend to mourn the impending death. We get the warning but do not know the date. When we learned of her diagnosis, it was already in significant stages and was progressing at an aggressive rate, so her time was limited. She passed within a few short months.

In that season of my life I was a few years out of college, figuring out my next steps with my degree and career while growing increasingly frustrated with God's demands over my life, disillusioned with career choices. At that point, I had given up a sport I loved (soccer), recovered from an ACL injury, worked a job I hated, and watched my peers live a YOLO (You Only Live Once) life. I felt I was missing out, and this Christian walk just was not worth it. I didn't want anything to do with Him and thought He was ruining my life. I was in shut down mode with God, but in hindsight, I was very much in transition and grieving the loss of my identity and failed dream to ride out my soccer career.

There I was, in a full blown backslide state with God, filled with regret and unprocessed grief, and I just did *not* want Him. I mean I was literally sitting in church under the preaching of sermons but not hearing them, nor was I remotely convicted or praying.

On one of those trips to my Tootz, we drove down and got to the hospital. Nothing could have prepared me for the sight. If you have ever lost someone to cancer, you understand how startling it is to see your loved one essentially be unrecognizable and borderline emaciated from the disease. In that hospital room, I didn't see the full lively Tati I remembered.

We gently tipped into the room so as not to disrupt her, and she looked over at us, smiled, and talked a little bit until she was tired. Then she asked for just me, my sister-in-law, and my infant niece to remain at her bedside and pray with her.

When she asked me to pray, I froze because it had been so long since I talked to Jesus. I literally couldn't say "no." Here is my tati, on her sick bed, dying and asking *me* to pray for her? As unworthy as I felt, there was no space of reality where a rebuttal of, "well actually listen Tati, me and God ain't seeing eye to eye right now sooooo..." Nope. Not an option. My sister-in-law looked at me to lead and my infant niece, cute as ever, instinctively silenced her own babbles in reverence. Then before I knew it, I took my tati's feeble hand and started to intercede like my life depended on it– because it did.

First, I immediately repented to God and asked the Lord to forgive me in that moment and succumbed to the divine encounter He wanted me to have with Him. He moved me, not to pray for her to live, but to pray His will be done in her life and His comfort to abound. That remains one of the most significant prayers I've ever prayed as an intercessor because I instantly felt His Holy spirit move to break up the fallow ground in me. I prayed myself into agreement with His will, even when it was contrary to my desire to want my aunt to live. My own will was also broken, and the heart of stone I worked up for so long was made into a heart of flesh when I went to Him to intercede on her behalf.

Who is God really to me?

My Tati loved the Lord until her dying breath and did not cease to encourage us in the scriptures even upon her hospital bed.
I remember feeling so overwhelmed with her transition as she was set up with hospice care in her home to be "comfortable" while I was thousands of miles away in New York. I felt this overwhelming feeling of helplessness, and the Lord dropped 2 Corinthians 4:16 to encourage me: "For which cause we faint not; but though our outward man perish, yet the inward man is renewed day by day."

He showed me that although outwardly cancer may be eating her flesh, inwardly her spirit man was being strengthened in and by Him. That was evidenced by Tati's unwavering commitment to Jesus in the face of suffering. I looked at my faithfully devoted

Tati, who was dying, in discomfort, and was not falsely charging God, instead her Faith was the strongest I've witnessed. Then verse 17 and 18 says,

> For our light affliction, which is but for a moment, worketh for us a far more exceeding and eternal weight of glory; While we look not at the things which are seen, but at the things which are not seen: for the things which are seen are temporal; but the things which are not seen are eternal.

The paradox of outwardly flesh wasting and inwardly being renewed and strengthened was not just to comfort me about my eventual destination, but it served as a reminder of our purpose on earth. My anger with God was because I believed He was depriving me of temporal pursuits when He wants a relationship with me (and you), and that is an eternal one. That is when the scales truly came off my eyes and I was able to step away from the pain of losing my aunt, realizing that I have the privilege of living in a relationship with God that will not leave nor forsake me (Deuteronomy 31:6). My mind then renewed to see that if He did not forsake my aunt in her time of affliction, surely He will not forsake me when I need Him.

She recited Psalm 119:17 constantly: "I shall not die, but live, and declare the works of the LORD." This woman believed wholeheartedly in her healing. And she did so live, as precisely as she should have, and her resolve in Christ– even in the face of cancer– was the mightiest declaration of them all. Her faith was so remarkable to me, especially when in the folly of my youth I couldn't fathom "wasting" any more of my youth serving Him. I firmly believe that He used my Tati Vivie's life, not only to be a testimony to others, but to transport me back into His arms of grace.

All this to say, while I was already in a state of progressive bitterness, compounding the loss of my aunt *nearly* put my heart in a place of disrepair. The intangibles added up slowly and surely, and before I knew it, my heart was adrift from God and hardened. But God! In His infinite mercy, He used the death of my aunt to jolt my faith to a resting place, just like the glorious hymn, "My Faith has Found a Resting Place" declares.

Whenever I think of that moment we prayed together, it brings tears to my eyes, not because of sadness, but because I remember God's faithfulness towards me and in my Tati's life, and I never want to forget the overwhelming feeling of that.

It is of the Lord's mercies that we are not consumed, because His compassions fail not.

Lamentations 3:22

Although I've incurred many losses since then, that one is poignant, for the single fact that it was the one that shook my faith entirely, exposed my theology, and confronted me with the question: who is God *really* to me? I allowed my heart to get hardened by disappointments, but with my aunt passing, that was the crossroads of my faith– where a decision had to be made.

Just as I was confronted in that moment, we all are, at some point, going to be in the face of loss with a similar question from God: *will we let our loss be the reason we abandon Him, or will we let Him intercede for us and trust Him?*

Lamentations 3:22-23 held more meaning after that decision: "It is of the Lord's mercies that we are not consumed, because his compassions fail not. They are new every morning: great is thy faithfulness." It was surely His mercy to redeem me in such a state! At the crux of my crisis was the fact that my belief system was dictating that the Lord was controlling my life, and seeing my frailing and emaciated Tati only added to what was there. When our loved ones are at death's door, we have no control, as we shouldn't. We are not God. However, if in our daily lives we are constantly competing with God to be (lowercase) *god* of our own lives, that natural helplessness will swiftly become or turn into a hardened heart. My erroneous theology at the time told me God is ruining my life; therefore, every subsequent event I would experience only contributed to that notion. When we harden our hearts, every offense is evidence and adds more concrete.

Although my aunt's battle with cancer was very real, the death of a loved one has this jarring ability to thrust us into an existential qualm about the life of a loved one and our own mortality. The combination of that mental burden is often what takes us down as we are processing it. There are also so many people, who after the loss of a loved one, walk away from God completely. For me, it provided the most ample opportunity to draw closer to Him.

When I reflect on that moment, it's one of those moments indelibly burned into my faith walk because I know the Holy Spirit spoke to my aunt when she asked me to pray for her. I may have asked God to give me the prayer to pray for her in her time of need, but little did she know (or maybe she did) that it was also my hour of need, too, as it proved to be the prayer that redeemed my soul and mind from a hardened place – from abandoning my heavenly father, the prayer that thrusted me back into His arms of grace. She was continually repeating "I will not die but live and declare the works of the Lord" (Psalm 118:17). That utterance was for her spirit man to live. That declaration was for me too. It was to not die a spiritual death; it was my call to live and go on to declare the works of the Lord.

I submit that my aunt did just that: her life and her faith– in the face of physical death– changed the course of my faith and that of the young women she mentored.

A hardened heart will blind us from seeing such grace abound. The enemy wanted me to stay exactly where I was, BUT GOD wanted me to be comforted in His arms. I didn't know that my aunt's death would be the vehicle for my faith to live and for many other young women whose lives she touched in the youth ministry. Her life preached the gospel until her last moments, and she left me with a legacy of tangible faith to go by. That is a priceless gift a hardened heart could never appreciate, that would scoff at, that would be offended by. Oh, but thanks be to God for giving me a heart of flesh that day so he could write on the tables of heart and I could receive Him again. My heart broke that day, but I rejoiced because I was able to *feel* again after being spiritually numb. A broken heart means it can be mended; fortunately, there is a God who specializes in broken pieces and making them whole.

Friend, what we don't see is how a hardened heart is surely death too. Declare, "I shall not die but live and declare the works of the Lord!" (Psalm 119). As much as we grieve, living a life *willfully* without God is a death in itself, *especially* when we know the truth. What we expend in anger towards God, He can fill but only after our hearts are tender, contrite, and inclined to Him. We are admonished in Hebrews 3:15, "Today if ye will hear His voice, harden not your hearts as in the provocation." Even more astounding is the fact that He used my aunt's transition to thrust me back into His arms of grace and back into relationship with Him. Ideally, that would not have been the course of events that I myself would have chosen to jolt me back into relationship with Him, but when I think back to the immense distance I drifted from Him in that season, He knew *precisely* what was needed to bring me back.

And so I urge you not to harden your heart because you are counting your losses; that ledger will surely only produce stone. When losses compound, we can be so accustomed to so much pain and loss in our life that we get callous and say, "Oh again? Fine." God does not want us to go through life on autopilot and emotionless; that is no way to live, neither is to be overtaken by every occurrence; however, we have to be mindful of how easy it is to total these experiences and file them away to never appear again. All we are doing is delaying the inevitable.

A hardened heart may appear to be impenetrable, but before it was hardened, there were particles and seeds that already went in before it was closed off. Being that it is not what goes into a man that defiles him but what comes out (Matthew 15:11), the abundance of the heart will spew what has gone in: pain.

Paul preaches on the power of Christ and the precision and liveliness of the Word of God. Like a plant in a fallow state, His word never dies out, even with our hardened heart and our grief. Hebrews 4:12-13 AMP says this about the living word of God:

> For the word of God is living and active *and* full of
> power [making it operative, energizing, and effective].
> It is sharper than any two-edged sword, penetrating
> as far as the division of the soul and spirit [the
> completeness of a person], and of both joints and
> marrow [the deepest parts of our nature], exposing *and*
> judging the very thoughts and intentions of the heart.
> And not a creature exists that is concealed from His
> sight, but all things are open *and* exposed, and revealed
> to the eyes of Him with whom we have to give account.

It is only the word of God, Christ Himself that can penetrate our hearts with such precision to produce an everlasting inclination towards Him.

Key Points:

- Disappointment does not happen overnight; it can develop after a culmination of losses that we do not process.

- A hardened heart from counting losses only produces stone.

- Only the word of God can penetrate our hearts (Hebrews 4:12-13).

Reflection & Exercise:

1. What is the moment that shook your faith to its core?

2. When you reflect, what about that moment disappointed you?

3. Where did you abandon God and where have you hardened your heart in this season? How have you reacted to that?

4. At this very moment, do you believe God is who He says He is? Why or why not?

5. Read Psalm 55 and find a verse that resonates with you.

Notes

Chapter 3

It's in God's Hands

3

It's in God's Hands

L oss is an eventuality that is the great equalizer. We know to expect it, yet when it occurs, it's no less surprising to learn once again we cannot control the timing, selection, nor severity of the loss. One of our biggest grievances with God we shutter to admit is his lack of permission concerning the things we perceive He takes. It also has a way of producing instantaneous humility because we have to acquiesce to reality, that we are *not* in control.

God in Himself is both omniscient (all-knowing) and Sovereign (Lord), meaning He can do as He will and nothing in our lives is a surprise to Him. Isaiah 46:10 says that He "declaring the end from the beginning, and from ancient times the things that are not yet done." God is well aware of our present losses because He willed it, and therefore, we can trust He knows precisely when and how we will overcome it.

In Psalm 31:15, King David even had to declare amidst difficulty that "my times are in your hands..." It is of consolation to know that God orchestrates all things and holds it together, and if my seasons in life are indeed in His most capable hands, then that is where they should be.

This is partly by design because there is only ONE God, and ONE Lord - Christ Jesus (1 Cor. 8:6).

Agree with God

Agreement is the balm to a hardened heart turned to flesh. It communicates that, "you are God and I am not." This is also the precursor to being able to receive His comfort because if we do not agree with His decision to take, to allow, to remove, and how He did so, then we have demonstrated by default that which we have lost– that person, that hobby, that job, that relationship– is our de facto idol.

He is a jealous God (Exod. 34:14), and that even means that in His providence, He decided to subtract *them* or *it*, while we remain to be refined. Now, that is not to say God is punitive because He "took" someone or something from us. That is the cry of a hardened heart. Making the confession of faith and accepting Salvation in Jesus Christ means that we accepted Him as Lord over our lives– the entirety of it. That confession was a covenant, one which is not predicated on the weather changing but backed with the full weight of His sacrifice on the cross for us. Loss is one of many trials we will traverse through in our process of sanctification to being more like Him. We may wonder, well how does loss make us more like Him, and why is this necessary?

...God desires too much wholeness in our lives for us to depreciate it by being angry at Him.

Simple: because He wills it.

When He shaped us (Ps. 119) and made our frame with intention, breathed His breath in us, saw fit to bring us into the world by way of our parents ... our permission was not a consideration then– *His* will was. He brought us forth for the purposes of Himself, not because God is selfish, but because we have a purpose on this earth and for His good pleasure. Like so, God made consideration of the exact circumstances in our lives. This, my friend, was one of the scenarios He accounted for, even before this moment, because He is from everlasting to everlasting.

Job's example

When we look in the Bible, some of the most notable stories related to loss and suffering are found in Job. In chapter one, after Job loses everything, this was his response:

> Then Job arose, and rent his mantle, and shaved
> his head, and fell down upon the ground, and
> worshipped... the Lord gave, and the Lord hath taken
> away; blessed be the name of the Lord
> (Job 1:20-21).

Job shows us an unconventional response to grief that is so contrary to everything that has been taken from him. Job recognized that the same God with the power to give those good things in our lives has the same power to remove them at His discretion. This revelation came after realizing the same God who graciously bestowed this person, opportunity, possession, etc., in our lives, and decided, in the counsel of His own will, to remove it or them. Next, in verse 21, he said "blessed be the name of the Lord." That is the agreement to say God is still God.

Now as we reflect up to this point, if we can say that, "all God seems to do in our life is continuously take," that language in itself reveals that we view God as a God who means to consistently punish us. That line of thinking is injurious to our faith, as we will then begin to take *every* loss in our lifetime and get stuck in being angry at God....God desires too much wholeness in our lives for us to depreciate it by being angry at Him. Another reason why we get stuck in anger is because we believe we are somehow owed an explanation for the loss or what was taken away. Because God's character is innately good, and He will not cease to be good because that is Him, and He can't not be who He is. The reality is that God is not the source of our angst– our disagreement with His sovereign plan is. This loss we experience is only spotlighting our dormant disagreement.

How is it that our example in Job, with all the cause in the world to curse God (as his friends taunted and hoped he would), did not charge God foolishly (Job 1:22)? As much as the loss will challenge theology in our lives, it will create a moment for us to experience Him, contrary to what we once believed Him as.

When I mention agreeing with God, it is not as though some magical switch goes off, but it is more of loosening our grasp from that which we loved. It is not as though our memories of the person wanes or their significance dies; it is that our agreement softens our resolve and acknowledgment of God's sovereignty, which becomes exalted over our circumstances. That is what agreement looks like: a loose grasp and a yielded heart, which is what he requires (Ps. 51:17).

Crushed soccer dreams

I started playing soccer at six years old when my dad and I would kick around the ball in our backyard for fun. In Haiti (as well as many countries outside the United States), soccer a.k.a. football is a way of life. My dad was never a professional player, but kicking the ball around was a carefree part of his childhood that he shared with me in our daddy-daughter time. Soccer was something that I was able to share with him, and with his encouragement, I went on to play for teams and became "Super G," a name my coaches gave me.

The joy was getting to play and leave all my emotions on the field. I experienced traveling to new states and the camaraderie of my teammates who had my back. I created memories, developed skills as a leader, and was a teamplayer. Soccer gave my life meaning. The better player I was, the more praise I received. It was reliable, it was constant, and it was "my thing" that I never dreamed of losing anytime soon, especially since I was recruited to play at the college level.

In my sophomore year of college, I experienced an ambiguous and tangible loss. During our last practice before the semi finals, I felt my knee pop, and the move I imagined doing stopped me short because of the excruciating pain in my knee. I knew then that I tore my ACL.

Now I've had plenty of injuries for the sake of the game, but I knew *instantly* this one was different. What sticks out to me from that day was not the physical pain of my knee, but the despair of my *dream* shattering in that movement. I seriously saw the montage of my soccer career play before me. If I'm being honest, my physical anguish was really exacerbated by my dreams of attaining soccer championships and personal glory slipping away. That is what had me exclaim in pain because the world as I knew it as being a star athlete dissipated.

With our medical advancements, ACL injuries are no longer the "career ending" injuries they used to be 20 plus years ago, so prior to surgery, I had a few options to consider on how to proceed with the repair and subsequent recovery schedule. Before the surgery, the Lord gave me clear instructions on which mode to select, and then he said to me, "G, you have the option to make this recovery experience pleasurable." This was God asking for my surrender to the process. Do you know we can be an obstacle to our own healing?

He told me this *before* any incision was made so I could prepare my mind for the recovery ahead because it would be more than physical– it would be spiritual and mental. Like many of us, the pain of our dream getting more distant to nonexistent can be equally grievesome. In the physical sense, that was getting tended to with corrective surgery and aids so I could simply walk, but intrinsically no *person* could tend to the ambiguous grief process that was needed; that was for me and God to work through.

Recovering from an injury or having to go to physical therapy can be incredibly humbling. In this instance, I literally had to learn to walk again, but that was synonymous to learning how to walk with Christ in the absence of what I thought was my identity (and as I learned, my idol). This was a vitally pivotal time in my faith because my injury was yet another accident, but this one challenged my identity. For my particular journey, I was not able to keep my idol and be who God wanted me to be. After having my tantrum, the work began. I had to allow God to expose what I really thought He *took* from me.

Thankfully, the recovery for my knee was very smooth. I cooperated with God, I surrendered. During that time, He revealed Himself to me, and I got my commission for who I would be in the body of Christ. Admittedly, having my dream seemingly snatched from me in that moment, right before the semi finals, where I was sure to shine as a starting center midfielder to bring my team and myself glory was startling. Recovery meant contending with "who am I if I'm not a soccer player?"

I hadn't really considered that before this point, especially because so much of my worth and affirmation came from being a soccer player.

It was a physical loss in the most obvious sense, but what went untended was the ambiguous loss of my dream because all of my youthly value was tied up in my soccer achievements. Had this event not occurred, I may have never recognized the unhealthy value I placed on my soccer career and performance. That moment shattered me and broke me down to pieces because I felt unfairly and unjustly robbed of *my* dream. Special emphasis on *my dream.* I am in no way saying dreams are wrong to have. What I missed then but know now is how small that dream was in comparison to what God wanted to do in my life and has done since (Jer. 29:11).

The reality is He gave me the faculties and coordination to play soccer and excel; had He wanted me to continue, then I would have. The real issue was that I had to confront myself in a way I never have and truthfully admit I did not like what was *left* of me when soccer was no longer in my life because I was superficially empty. In my case, it was a swift and painful loss because I mistakenly clung to soccer tighter than I clung to my Savior. Had He not graciously ordained for me to experience that loss, I wouldn't have embraced *His* life assignment for me.

Cultivating agreement

> *Before I was afflicted I went astray: but now have I*
> *kept thy word. Thou art good and doest good teach*
> *me thy statutes... it is good for me that I have been*
> *afflicted; that I might learn thy statutes.*
> *(Ps. 119: 67-68, 71)*

These three verses hold significant meaning in cultivating agreement because before my affliction, I was proud and boastful in my soccer superstardom and being a starting player. Afterwards, I was humbled and it became good ground to hear and learn God's will for my life. I couldn't hear it– couldn't hear Him– over my pride.

In Psalm 119: 65, it reads "Thou hast dealt well with thy servant, O Lord according to thy word." That is the language of agreement. In God's decision, He did well. When God takes, it doesn't feel pleasurable, but when it settles– because we belong to Him– we can't help but agree. I have been incapacitated enough through affliction to where I have undoubtedly learned to sit still and to testify that He does indeed deal well with His servant. Even Christ learned obedience through the things he suffered

Our agreement is an eventuality.

(Heb. 5:8-9). Jesus was perfect because he did not sin, and he fully demonstrated his submission to God. Submission, even in a hard situation and in the face of loss, is where the Holy Spirit has latitude to work. That is the sweet savour God can work with. As one commentary says, "real obedience is obeying God even when it costs us something."[2]

The affliction of despair, disappointment, dejection, sorrow– you name it– that ensued after the transition or loss was a necessary course for our covenant with God. Now we can *delight* in his law more than we exalted the ache of the void.

Because it is written that, "Every knee will bow and every tongue will confess that Jesus is Lord," our agreement is an eventuality (Phil. 2: 10-11). If we are saved, we confess that God is within His rights to do as He will with His creation because as Lord, it is at His discretion to do so. Then, in Psalm 119:65, David acknowledges his position as a servant: lowly, yet appreciative of how God has been gracious regardless. The "before" he refers to in verse 67, he lacked understanding; *before* lacked the fruit of discipline; *before* lacked perspective, but now we can stand in the fruit of the good from that specialized school of affliction.

Perhaps what was lost could very well be what was leading us astray and/or had the propensity to, which is why God, in His sovereignty, chose to remove it. At the end of the day, He is both a jealous God and the lover of our souls. Because He is from everlasting to everlasting, He knows that for the interest of our souls and those things or people that had to be removed in order for us to keep the law. His good is not *our* good. To appreciate verse 71, "it *is*" good, David is standing in the byproduct of His goodness after being afflicted, which tells us sometimes we cannot appreciate the affliction until *after* it happens.

All of this to say, our agreement with the decision is what will dictate the course of our healing from this wound and void in our lives. Agreement looks like, "you are still God, even when I don't get what I want." Just like when we came into salvation, we had to acknowledge Him as Lord. Here again in the valley, we must also acknowledge Him as Lord over this decision even when we can't see it yet. That alone requires a measure of faith that feels supernatural, especially considering how much that thing meant to us.

Key Points:

- Loss is the great equalizer.

- Agreement is the precursor to being able to receive His comfort.

- Agreement softens our resolve and acknowledges God's sovereignty.

- Agreement looks like a loose grasp and a yielded heart (Ps. 51:17).

Reflection & Exercise:

1. What/who are you holding on to that God may want you to let go for your good?

2. Who does God say you are without it? Write down three scriptures to accompany this belief.

3. Like Job, what moment has this loss created for you to experience God?

4. What do you believe it will cost you if you do not agree?

5. Picture the other side of your loss. What does it look like to fully agree in this area?

Notes

Chapter 4

Fixing Our Eyes on God

4

Fixing Our Eyes on God

If you've ever been to a state fair or carnival in your childhood, there is a ride called the *Gravitron* or Round-up. The Round-Up is a large circular platform with caged walls that people stand against. The platform spins, and then the arm that holds the platform raises up, so the ride is tilted. The tops of the walls are secured by cables which connect to an object in the center of the platform that doubles as a center ornament, although some rides have axed the ornamental pieces altogether. The spots where riders stand against have a thin padding and riders are 'secured' by a chain link. On this circular ride, you're standing against an angled wall vertically in a panel while the ride progressively increases speed, spinning and the platform simultaneously rises up and down.

When boarding, you select your spot and secure yourself, and during the ride while in your individual panel, the force from gravity pushes you against the padding of the wall. It is a fun challenge to see how much you can move, all to succumb to the force of gravity which prevents you from moving and even turning your head. Once the ride finishes and the operator brings it to a halt, the walk out of your panel is disorienting, but in the name of "fun" you move on to the next adventure.

> **Beyond acknowledging, accepting, and submitting, the next most important thing we must do is shift our gaze from who or what we have lost to the Lifter of our Heads.**

Similarly, the intensity of our despair can make it hard to focus. Grief is disorienting: we may think we've selected the right slot which can be a career, role, or relationship, and the forces of life, operated by The Operator (God), shows us rather quickly we have no control of this ride of life.

Beyond acknowledging, accepting, and submitting, the next most important thing we must do is shift our gaze from who or what we have lost to the Lifter of our Heads (Psalm 3:3). We are grieving without hope or without a savior. The Bible tells us in 1 Thessalonians 4:13 NIV, "Brothers and sisters, we do not want you to be uninformed about those who sleep in death, so that you do not grieve like the rest of mankind, who have no hope."

A benefit of salvation is that we have hope in Christ and that there is more to this life beyond the temporal, and because of His efficacious sacrifice, we have *hope* in Him. I say that to say He is a God that is big enough to handle the depth of our despair and longing for that which was lost. Here in this very moment is where we have the ability to put our emotions on the strength of God's character because He *can* handle it. He is *not* a friend or a spouse who has a limited attention span and zones out the moment we share our hearts, nor is He a God that is aloof to our emotions. Jeremiah 23:23 says, "Am I a God at hand, saith the Lord, and not a God afar off?" Meaning, He is not only near, he is present whatever the distance. It is so easy to feel locked into the onslaught of feelings as though we have no outlet. Much like David when he cried out in Psalm 13:1-6 NLT:

> O LORD, how long will you forget me? Forever?
> How long will you look the other way? How long
> must I struggle with anguish in my soul, with sorrow
> in my heart every day? How long will my enemy have
> the upper hand? Turn and answer me, O LORD my
> God! Restore the sparkle to my eyes, or I will die.
> Don't let my enemies gloat, saying, "We have defeated
> him!" Don't let them rejoice at my downfall. But I
> trust in your unfailing love. I will rejoice because you
> have rescued me. I will sing to the LORD because he
> is good to me.

Sometimes we are so caught up in our own feelings, it is all we rehearse– the betrayal, the removal, the passing– that we feel so bruised we cannot fathom a moment beyond it. The longer we do, the more time warps and we are ensnared by those very feelings. That, my friend, is a cry of defeat.

The operative part being our own selves, although our feelings are entirely valid because of the significance of the loss, it isn't beneficial to stay there, nor is that God's intent. That is the enemy.

Anguish is a deep form of wrestling with ourselves that has almost no articulation to it; we just feel it to the very core and depth and know our hearts are broken. When I recount my most difficult seasons, I had hardly any words, but to my core I was wounded. It's also so overwhelming that it can be difficult to navigate how to come out of it. So, when David is talking about that *daily* struggle in Psalm 13, it is a depiction of how sorrow can just be lodged there uncomfortably, and yet has somehow taken up residence. Sorrow has then become too comfortable and the norm.

God can handle our emotions

Remember the story of Job? Remember He lost *everything*: family, lands, all of it within a day. And while he spoke with his so-called friends or accusers, he captured the depth of his own pain: "Yet if I speak, my pain is not relieved; and if I refrain, it does not go away" (Job 6:6 NIV).

It's like we're stuck. The longer we fixate on who or what we have lost, the harder it becomes to receive the help from the One true and living God who loves us. To fix our eyes, we must first fix our heart. It is a posture and decision. The same heart that was broken is the very same that we must give back to God to mend. Therefore, this requires active participation on our part (with the help of the Holy Spirit) to turn from the counsel of *our* own soul and to *His* unfailing love (v. 6). David said "I will rejoice" and "I trust." How does one go from such deep anguish to trust? The difference here is that the anguish was self-centered. The trust is now God-centered because we don't trust in our *own* heart; we trust in God's "unfailing love." Our hearts are prone to fail and our feelings are prone to lie, but God's love for us is big enough, strong enough, enduring enough to both cover and supersede the anguish. My my my!

The natural solution is to dwell on the loss; the necessary solution is to give it to God. The vitality of our healing is tied to our gaze. Will we gaze on the loss, or will we fix our eyes on His perfect, unfailing love towards us in the midst?

Living in sorrow daily is not the life God desires for us. He came so that we can live life and live it more abundantly (John 10:10), not to just be the product of circumstance and be continually defeated by it.

> Therefore if you have been raised with Christ [to a new life, sharing in His resurrection from the dead], keep seeking the things that are above...Set your mind and keep focused habitually on the things above [the heavenly things], not on things that are on the earth [which have only temporal value] (Col. 3:1-2 AMP).

When the Bible tells us to set our affections on things above, that is because the things of this earth are temporal and will pass away. The company will restructure, organizations will shift, we will outgrow relationships, move, and change – that is a guarantee, but if we remember in whom we trust and where our value lies, keeping our mind on heavenly things is the antidote to our sorrow. As we have seen, hoarding our sorrow only amplified the same sorrow. Why not magnify God instead?

Interestingly, when we are hurt, we don't want anyone to touch it. We bump our heads, the first thing we do is *cover* it. Our nature is to cover our pain and hide it. We will hide from family, friends, colleagues, and the like all to "save face," when in reality, we are only causing more injury to ourselves. Perhaps it's because the track record or history of people were fickle and they dropped the ball a few times, but that is not

When we fix our eyes on God, we fix our eyes toward Him, who is our hope and the Lifter of our heads...

the God we serve. He is far more attentive and His ear is always inclined to us.

Likewise, we need a nurse or another person to apply first aid because they have a better view of the injury and the remedies at their disposal to administer the aid. God Himself is the One with the entire view of our hearts and is ready to administer aid at our behest, but we have to *look* for Him and acknowledge we need Him to do so.

We also try to distract ourselves from pain because it's honestly far easier to focus on just about anything else. When I admonish us to fix our eyes on God, it's not as a means of distraction as much as doing so is a focal point for *hope*. When we fix our eyes on God, we fix our eyes toward Him, who is our hope and the Lifter of our Heads, fixing our eyes on the emblem of our faith when it is rocky.

Had Christ not fixed his eyes on the cross, he wouldn't have gone to Calvary for us. That reminds me of Psalm 3:3, where David called God the "Lifter of His Head." Surely in the depths of despair and persecution, we need an external force to give us hope. In the garden of Gethsemane, Jesus asked if the cup could pass three times (Matt. 26:39). He fully acknowledged His emotion while acquiescing to His Father's will. The agony of that weight hit him because it meant separation from His Father for carrying the penalty of our sin. Fortunately for us, on this side of salvation, we are not without hope and can put the entirety of our emotions on God– He is equipped to handle it all. Nor do we have to do it without Him, hallelujah! Since we have free will, we absolutely have the choice to fix our hope on plenty of other things or people while we grieve; however, we will soon learn that it is empty and will only distract, not lift.

Additionally, we can only be lifted when we know to whom we are lifting our eyes. His character is what gives credence and credibility to His impeccable track record as the lifter of our heads. There is a song called "Our Eyes Are Still On You" by John W.

Stevenson that I loved hearing in church.[3] These lyrics come to mind:

> *Lord, we acknowledge you*
> *we don't know what to do*
> *but our eyes are on you.*
>
> *We have not been this way,*
> *each step is strange and new,*
> *But our eyes are on you.*
>
> *Teach us your ways and we will follow*
> *speak to us now and we'll obey,*
> *You've always brought us through*
> *Our eyes are still on you.*

Feel free to replace the "we" with "I" to personalize it, but the sentiments are that of a heart posture acknowledging God for his Lordship. The scariness that is going through a new season, then reliance on His character, to the refrain that "our eyes are *still* on God." When we take a moment to recount His faithfulness in *every* season of our lives, this season of grief may be unusual, but God is unchanging and constant. In no way am I dubbing us "professional grievers," nor is that a title we'd like to have; however, even in the uncertainty, our eyes are on Him, looking to the hills from where our help comes from (Ps. 121:1), which means we are fixed in the right direction.

Grief doesn't have to be for us a "pulling up of your own bootstraps" endeavor; that is for the self-reliant. Just like the song says to "teach us your ways," we need God to guide us through our grief. Compared to being in a classroom with an instructor in the front of the room, we, as good students, are attentive to the instruction of the teacher for the lesson. Likewise, there is both a lesson and guidance in the season of grief we find ourselves in that can come only by the instruction of the Master Teacher, and it is He on whom we fix our eyes and our hope.

Key Points:

- We must shift our gaze from who or what we have lost to the Lifter of our Heads (Ps. 3:3).

- God's love for us is big enough, strong enough, enduring enough to both cover and supersede our anguish.

- When we fix our eyes on God, we fix our eyes toward Him.

Self Reflection & Exercise:

1. Take a minute to reflect and truly ask, where have you been fixing your eyes other than on God?

2. How have you been hiding your pain?

3. In what ways have you been relying on yourself?

4. How can you shift that responsibility back to God?

5. Read Psalm 121 and declare it over yourself. Which verse speaks to you most?

Notes

Chapter 5

God's Peace and Comfort are Unmatched

5

God's Peace and
Comfort are Unmatched

The word 'comfort', according to the International Standard Bible Encyclopaedia, means "to console, to encourage and strengthen by consolation."[4] The Greek word for comfort is *parakaleo*, which has an etymological meaning, 'to call alongside of,' i.e. to summon for assistance.[5] To comfort is to cheer and encourage. It has a positive force in its synonym "console," as it indicates the dispelling of grief by the impartation of strength. Additionally, the Holy Spirit has a similar Greek translation– *paraclete*, which translates to advocate, counsellor, or helper.[6]

My Father! We have an advocate in the Holy Spirit, which is dispensed to us to walk alongside us and aid us as we grieve. We cannot receive an impartation of comfort from God by way of his Holy Spirit (Himself) without acknowledging who He is.

How awesome is it that we serve a God who is ready and willing to walk alongside us as we grieve!

Many of us don't even realize we are grieving something because it's not a conventional loss. It takes the Holy Spirit to show us and also prompt us back into His arms. There is a reason why we were promised a Savior in Jesus, who is also referred to as the Wonderful Counselor. He is our Prince of Peace. It is crucial for us to call Him by not only who He is but who we need Him to be in our season. Isaiah 9:6 tells us, "For to us a Child shall be born, to us a Son shall be given; And the government shall be upon His shoulder, And His name shall be called Wonderful Counselor, Mighty God, Everlasting Father, Prince of Peace."

It takes the Wonderful Counselor to minister to our hearts afresh and mend the brokenness, a Mighty God to lift our head, an Everlasting Father to both endure and remain, and a Prince of Peace to calm the crashing waves of despair after loss. That is the kind of God who is ready to walk alongside us at this very moment. The enemy wants us to believe we are grieving alone, but that is not so! The Prince of Peace is on point, unlike others who are fickle; when we call upon Him, he answers.

In sorrow, so much is out of our control, particularly the season which is far from our choice, but what we *can* do is elect to receive His perfect peace. Rejecting the peace and comfort He is ready to dispense only leaves us empty. As His creation, we have a god-shaped hole that only He can fill. We err when we look for substances, people, and things to fill it.

Blessed are they that mourn

> *Blessed are they that mourn: for they shall be comforted (Matt 5:4).*

We are all familiar with Matthew 5, the Beatitudes, where Jesus shares a series of "blessed" promises that speaks to the experiences reserved for those who belong to the kingdom of God. In verse four, He speaks specifically to those who are mourning and promises the assurance that they will receive comfort. This is not just a cavalier saying to be overlooked; it is a promise because he said it. In the Bible, within the New Testament, there's the Synoptic Gospels written by his disciples Matthew, Mark, Luke, and John recounting Jesus's ministry, where the lettering in red indicates that Jesus said it. Now, while the entire Bible is God-inspired, it is of special note that Jesus said those highlighted words directly. We will also find that because He came to fulfill the law, it can be cross referenced to Old Testament scripture as well.

That being so, the pattern in the Beatitudes is that Jesus will call out those in that particular circumstance followed by the antidote to that circumstance. I also find it fascinating that he first calls us "blessed." The noun, *makarios*, in Greek here which according to Strong's concordance translates to "supremely blessed; by extension, fortunate, well off, happy." [7] We are pronounced blessed to mourn, fortunate even.

Understandably, this is probably quite hard to conceive that in the midst of loss that we'd be considered blessed when fortune or happiness is not yet in view. However, Jesus is very intentional in what he says when saying, "are they," He is speaking to our state in Him. Jesus' pronouncement of our standing being blessed in His eyes while we're grieving. Moreover, the word *mourn* is used here.[8] In this particular verse, it is used as an intransitive verb, which does not specify a thing or object. I take that as whatever has brought us to the state of mourning and grief has also brought us to His feet, which is why we are blessed because there, and with Him, is where we can receive His comfort. We are blessed to grieve because we have a Savior who is and acts as our comforter and *the* source of the comfort promised. What a wonderful Savior we have that we do not have to grieve alone! This verse speaks to the assurance we have that comfort *is* our portion when we inevitably find ourselves in a season of lament. The work was finished on the cross for us when He shed His blood, and

He can fully fill the cracks of our broken hearts and will go into the unseen parts to excavate and heal.

because we serve an all-knowing God, He has all authority to, as the Sovereign King who we submit to, pronounce us blessed before we even experience it. When the season arises, He calls us fortunate because He has the remedy.

In God's loving arms

> Psalm 73:26: *"My flesh and my heart faileth: but God is the strength of my heart, and my portion forever."*

Has your heart ever been so broken it just aches from the want of the person or thing lost, which at first it pierces then it dulls? This psalm reminds me of that state because the extent of our ability proves woefully inadequate. When we get to that state or the end of ourselves is where we are now perfectly suited to receive His strength. Our frailty, our sorrow, and our despair signals a readiness for His strength which will come in the form of comfort and consolation. When we realize we don't have to be "strong" or act like we have it all together is when we can be postured to receive supernatural strength to continue. "Faileth" in Hebrew *kālâ* translates to being spent, used up, to be exhausted.[9] Here is where we are permitted to be undone in His presence.

Psalm 56:8 MSG says, "You've kept track of my every toss and turn through the sleepless nights, each tear entered in your ledger, each ache written in your book." His comfort does not absolve us from the pangs of pain, but it does act as a divine balm. His name alone heals *all*, broken hearts included.

There are things and people I have lost that I couldn't conceive living without at the time in my limited understanding, but praise be to God! I am yet living, not by my own strength, but by the One who is the strength of my heart (and yours too). He is our portion and has everything we need. He can fully fill the cracks of our broken hearts and will go into the unseen parts to excavate and heal. His comfort cannot be compared to even our most beloved loved one; He far supersedes that in a supernatural way. It must be *super* to our *nature* because we can't conceptualize what life would look like after this.

Once we have experienced the comfort of God, we won't be as ready to jump into the arms of others because it's unlike any other experience we've had. It's like being wrapped in the coziest blanket and drinking a cup of warm hot chocolate. We are lifted and mended simultaneously, though not in one shot, but it takes intention to dwell and sit with it. God doesn't get exhausted by us, nor is our sorrow or sadness a burden to Him. He pours out His comfort from a reservoir of living waters that never runs out or dries up. We all know someone in our lives who gives amazing hugs, like the kind of hug that makes us feel warm all over, full and lifted. His comfort exceeds that infinitely!

The deeper our pain, the more we should hasten our footsteps to the throne where our father awaits us with open arms.

When my Tati Vivie passed away, I remember feeling the need to be strong because I saw how everyone else was completely undone. It's not that I wasn't sad, but I was inexplicably also not overtaken. I attribute that to the peace and comfort I received in my secret place with God. I vividly recall receiving hugs from some family members and just not feeling any better. In my mind, my aunt was still gone, and I was left with a flurry of emotions I had not yet unpacked. Those feelings weighed heavy because the Wonderful Counselor had not yet arrived for me.

The thing is we do not have to wait to experience His comfort and peace; it is in these precise moments during our trials or when calamity is at our door that we ought to go to Him. The deeper our pain, the more we should hasten our footsteps to the throne where our father awaits us with open arms. We don't press because we have no other recourse, but because He is whom our soul longs for. How awesome is it that all His devotion and affection is fixed on us during trials? When wholeness feels elusive and tears are our meat day and night, the depth of our sorrow and despair is evidence that we need a Savior (Ps. 42:5). When loss has left me empty, God has lavishly poured out His love over me. When our mind is overwhelmed, peace is the portion we should seek. I believe that is what Paul was referring to in Philippians 4:7 NIV when he says, "And the peace of God, which transcends all understanding, will guard your hearts and your minds in Christ Jesus." It is indescribable and incomparable, yet fully satisfying. This is what I desire for us: to feel the fullness of His embrace in our hour of need.

Let's also remember Romans 8:38-39 AMP which says,

> For I am convinced [and continue to be convinced—
> beyond any doubt] that neither death, nor life, nor
> angels, nor principalities, nor things present and
> threatening, nor things to come, nor powers, nor
> height, nor depth, nor any other created thing, will be
> able to separate us from the [unlimited] love of God,
> which is in Christ Jesus our Lord.

So, we should ask ourselves: are we, too, fully persuaded, or will we let this loss keep us from fully experiencing the love and comfort that awaits us?

I come to encourage myself (and you) that there is life after this, and God will wrap us up in His arms while gently holding the fragments of our hearts. That is why He is the lifter of our heads. When the burden of loss is too hard to bear in our strength, when we toss and turn in that sleepless night, He makes up the difference and takes it on *for* us. Let us unburden ourselves today; let him carry them and us. The heaviness of the heart is not our portion.

Key Points:

- The Holy Spirit (*paraclete*) is an Advocate, Counsellor, & Helper.

- We do not have to wait to experience His comfort and peace.

- The peace of God is indescribable and incomparable, yet fully satisfying (Phil. 4:7).

Self Reflection & Exercise:

1. When it comes to being comforted by God, what comfortable act or item would you compare it to?

2. Who hugs you with the love of God that makes your spirit feel warm, full, and lifted?

3. What is keeping you from fully experiencing the love and comfort waiting for you?

4. Read Psalm 30 and reflect: what was your mourning into dancing moment?

5. Sit quietly for a few minutes, invite God's presence in the room, and ask Him to come alongside you. Remember what that feels like.

Notes

_____

_____

_____

_____

_____

_____

_____

_____

_____

_____

Chapter 6

Loss is Gain

6

Loss is Gain

One of my favorite preachers of the gospel, Bishop Jacqueline McCullough, says that "God is a wise economist," in that He never wastes a season or experience in our life. Just as Job exclaimed in Job 1:21, "He gives and takes away, blessed be the name of the Lord," God is God alone; therefore, we must come to a resolve in that a thing or person we have no longer present, or what we have is because he graciously allows it to be so. In allowing this season of loss in our lives, it is designed to extricate praise that otherwise would not occur except through this specific trial. Whatever He takes away is because it's not needed or has served its purpose; whatever remains currently serves a purpose, and whatever He adds is exactly what we need. Consider also that what loss has graciously deducted or subtracted is not to the point of deficit; we are not at zero. Christ is the remainder because even if we have nothing, we still have everything in Him.

God's omniscience + God's subtraction = purposeful gain

All of God's subtractions or deductions have purpose to them. Where we err is centralizing what or *who* we lost more than who remains– our God, our Father Jesus who will never leave us nor forsake us (Deut. 31:6). It takes a concerted effort, or rather, a supernatural grace to shift our gaze from our loss back to our Father. John 3:30 AMP states, "He must increase [in prominence], but I must decrease." The act of decreasing when God is involved looks like humility. It is the subtraction of knowingness, understanding we are not in this equation because God is God, and we allow Him to do what He does best.

Much of what we incur in loss is for us to be able to produce. This is what our lives are for: to be a reflection of Him and produce fruit on this earth. When we look at God's math pertaining to our losses, the more of God we make room for. By way of losses is how He can make Himself great and known in our sorrow and our healing. Not to say all things are bad that have felt stripped or taken from us, but there is foreknowledge by God for what had the potential to become an idol in our lives and what had the propensity to be more "prominent" than that of Jesus. John the Baptist had it right by giving the disclaimer that although he's done the works he was sent to, his role was to make room for Christ. Likewise, our losses have a way of making room for Him, too. That job that we dedicated 60 hours a week to and agonized over, yet had no time to do a devotional? Gone. That relationship that had us acting out of character, pulling us back to old habits, and forgetting who we were in Christ? Over. That car that was totaled because it was

Once again, by subtraction, He still makes room to get glory.

a vanity purchase? No more. The list can go on, but think for a moment and reflect now that we have the gift of hindsight. Many of those things were beneficial for a season but ultimately no longer a necessity.

We also have to think of the loved one who is no longer here who wasn't "a bad person" or harming us. They could be a loving parent or grandparent or uncle, yet and still, in God's sovereignty, He ultimately decided that their time in our lives expired, and we received all we were supposed to in the period of time they were here. Moreover, our time to impart or pour into that relationship, job, or that expensive car has run its course. God accounted for the entirety of our relationship and the seeds sown, and allows all parties to receive the healing of that loss. Praise God for that.

Remember, the posture of agreement will say the time allotted was sufficient, amen. Even if the relationship wasn't on the best of terms per se, it was sufficient. Psalm 27:10 says, "When my father and my mother forsake me, then the Lord will take me up." This scripture presupposes that there is an appointed time God has factored in for our loved ones to forsake us in this life while they are here, yet it is fully accounted for by God because that is when He is ready to take us up. Whether the forsaking is in the natural by their human actions or by death, the God of our salvation is fully prepared to do what He does

He is worth all that we give up and more for the purpose He has given our lives...

best: comfort. Once again, by subtraction, He still makes room to get glory. This is not because He is a cold and calculating or egotistical God. Though yes, He is a jealous God –and rightfully so– as we are commanded to have no other Gods beside or above Him (Exod. 20:3-5), but He is also Jehovah Shammah, the Present God.

Loss and gain in the Bible

The Apostle Paul was a pharisee before converting to Christianity, so his encounters with loss and gains for God aren't taboo when he masterfully speaks of this topic for us in Philippians 3:7-10:

> But what things were gain to me, those I counted loss for Christ. Yea doubtless, and I count all things but loss for the excellency of the knowledge of Christ Jesus my Lord: for whom I have suffered the loss of all things, and do count them but dung, that I may win Christ, And be found in him, not having mine own righteousness, which is of the law, but that which is through the faith of Christ, the righteousness which is of God by faith: That I may know him, and the power of his resurrection, and the fellowship of his sufferings, being made conformable unto his death[...]

Here, Paul is referring to his past privileges afforded to him from his status as a Jew during his time persecuting the Church, thinking he was earning merit with God. The Greek translation of "gain" here is *kérdos*, as a noun meaning advantage.[10] The next term, "count" *hēgéomai*, the Greek translation means to consider, deem, account, think.[11] Finally, *zēmía*, meaning detriment, damage, loss.[12]

As we know a noun to be a person, place, or thing, Paul illustrates to us in Philippians how all the "things" before that added to his identity. When he recounted and considered his loss, those things were actually more of a detriment to him because ultimately, all must be given up for Christ. He is worth all that we give up and more for the purpose He has given our lives, and what we lost is no comparison to the purpose and meaning Christ has now ascribed to our lives by being in Him (v.7). Paul was able to put those things on the other side of the ledger because he found utmost gain in the knowledge of the excellency of Christ Jesus. That kind of knowledge is only gained through experiencing an intimate companionship and communion with Christ (Phil. 3:8 AMP).

Then in verse 8 (b clause) in other versions is translated to, "For Whose sake I have *been caused* to forfeit..." Now when he counts or tallies, Paul willingly forfeits because the real accounting or *hēgéomai* is that next to Christ, everything is nothing. For what cause? Verse 10 says, "That I may know him, and the power of his resurrection, and the fellowship of his sufferings, being made conformable unto his death..." And there it is: the ultimate gain to our life is in our faith of what Christ did on the cross for us. The difference in what we count as a loss is what God decides it is. This type of *hēgéomai* (count) considers Christ where, by the lens of faith and the assurance in whom we believe, the *kérdos* (things) must be *zēmía* (loss). It is not to say everything in our lives is a loss, but now that we *consider* Christ differently, we accept what He has decided would be detrimental and *agree* with it.

The many ways we gain
We have discussed loss and gain, but what does that really look like? What do we get out of looking to Christ as we go through a season of loss? The following are a few areas of consideration when it comes to gaining in the season of loss.

Salvation or rededication to Christ
I've heard it said that eulogies are not given for the deceased but for the living. When we lose someone and the eulogizer reads the story of their life, it is often an account of how they lived their life on earth– accolades, who they are survived by, impact of their

life's work, and a semblance of hope to the loved ones. Death has a way of making us confront our own mortality, the finality of death, and the legacy we can potentially leave behind. This offers an opportunity for introspection and for us to evaluate what we are doing with our lives and what our destination could be.

Personally, after attending several family member's funerals consecutively, it made me more grateful to know my standing in Christ and grateful to be saved. It provides another level of comfort knowing we will eventually be with our Father in heaven; however, if you have not yet come to that conclusion for yourself, I invite you to consider that this season may be how God intends to draw you to (or back to) Himself. I also shared my own encounter earlier where I rededicated my life to Christ after the passing of my beloved Tati Vivie. I remember at her funeral, several young ladies who she mentored in her youth ministry group gave their lives to Christ. That is legacy and that is gain for the kingdom of God. I sincerely praise God for that encounter and for His mercy in using her passing as part of my own scheduled divine encounter to this day.

For some of us, having to grapple with our existential frailties is precisely the conditions that merit our surrender and acceptance of Christ, for Jesus is the ultimate gain. If you identify with this too, and you want to accept Jesus Christ as your Savior, you can pray these words to God in accordance to Romans 10:8-9 with me:

Prayer:

*Heavenly Father,
I come before You today, acknowledging my
shortcomings and my need for Your grace and
forgiveness.*

*I believe that Jesus Christ is Your Son—that He died on
the cross for my sins and rose again so that I might have
new life in Him.*

*I repent of my past and humbly invite
You into my heart.*

Please be my Lord and Savior.

*Lead me, direct my steps, and help me to live in a way
that honors You.*

*Thank You for Your love, Your mercy,
and the gift of a new beginning.*

*In Jesus' Name I pray,
Amen.*

**Remember: It's not the words that save you but your faith in Jesus and
what He did on the cross. This prayer is just a way to express that faith.*

Spiritual perception

Have you ever been to the optometrist for a vision exam?

When you go to the back with the doctor, they sit you behind a flat apparatus that you press your face against with magnifiers over your eyes to look at the chart for the visual acuity and refraction testing. The doctor then proceeds to toggle between lenses and ask, "One or two? Which is clearer?" And it continues until you are able to read through the chart to the smallest line to determine your acuity and an aspirational 20/20 score. The intention is to give you as much clarity and power to get to 20/20. Similarly, as we navigate grief, the affliction acts as its own unique corrective lens and purifier of sorts from low clarity lenses of pain to get us closer to seeing God for *who He is*, not what He takes. Now with hindsight, when we come through this season, we will see it was for our good.

Let's also Remember Saul's (Paul) conversion experience on the Damascus road in Acts 9. He was knocked off his horse, and as verse 8a (AMP) describes, " Saul got up from the ground, but though his eyes were open, he could see nothing..." Later on, the Lord sends the prophet Ananias to restore Saul's sight, and when he laid hands to do so, scales fell from his eyes and he immediately received his sight, got up, and got baptized (v.18). Knowing Saul's intention to persecute the church and his history, this conversion thrusted him out of his own plans and schemes and into direct obedience. In his natural sight, all he could see was his rage before him and God interrupted that to give him new sight spiritually.

This demonstrates that it's possible to have open eyes and yet no sight. Saul had eyes but no perception when he was knocked down, but when he got up, he was able to recognize God afresh and then obey immediately. My God, before we experienced our loss, we saw the world one way, but it took God Himself to upset our plans to give us the spiritual perception to perceive what He is doing beyond our natural sight. Grief causes us to check our perception because spiritual sight is a byproduct of faith. Now, we are able to see more of Him and less of us.

Protection

Naturally, it's hard to conceive how loss could equate to protection when we insolate ourselves by what and who we accumulate. As God subtracts, He decides what is beneficial to our lives and, in turn, what cannot continue with us into the next season. Truly, it is of His mercies we are not consumed (Lam. 3:22-23), and in rearranging our life priorities, He also mercifully keeps us from ourselves and our propensity to encroach perilously close to the idolatry of our lowercase *gods*. If we're honest, some of the people and things that we no longer have were in that category. On this side, we can be grateful for His mercy in the removal.

Grief causes us to check our perception because spiritual sight is a byproduct of faith.

Identity & Purpose

One would think at our big age we already have a solid concept of who we are, right? Through the stripping of our accoutrements that we propped up and people we used to eclipse who God has called us to be is when we can see God more clearly. We, in turn, begin to see ourselves through His eyes.

Exodus 20:3-5 AMP:

> You shall have no other gods before Me. You shall
> not make for yourself any idol, or any likeness (form,
> manifestation) of what is in heaven above or on the
> earth beneath or in the water under the earth [as an
> object to worship]. You shall not worship them nor
> serve them; for I, the Lord your God, am a jealous
> (impassioned) God [demanding what is rightfully and
> uniquely mine]...

Each area in which I've experienced loss brought me to this
moment and to this page with you right now. That is a purposeful
burden I wouldn't otherwise have, had it not been for Him using
those seasons for me to bring you the words on this page today.

Trust & Obedience

As I mentioned earlier, grief has a way of exposing our theology
and what we believe of God, how we handle this season, and how
we trust God demonstrates to Him what He can also trust us with.
We grow in trust with God so He can, in turn, trust us. When we
go through a valley and come out with the same God who brought
us through it, and realize it was Him, not people, that kept us,
our trust in Him grows. With every loss, I have learned to lean in
before I recline in my own understanding which has always been
regressive. This level of trust produced in this season coupled with
an unmistakable encounter increases our adoration.

While navigating losses, it also helps us to be quicker to obedience because we understand now that life is vapor and what we
hold to sometimes may not be what God wants us to have when
he decides it. As these seasons show us that, that hastens our knees
to bow.

Prayer & Worship

Prayer is where we retreat to the safety of God's ear to communicate with Him. These encounters cause us to pray differently in that we find ourselves increasing our dialogue with God. There is more depth to them, as well as our endurance to pray longer. I've been a culprit of some "drive by" prayers, (which can serve their purpose), but having gone through the

In every situation [no matter the circumstances] be thankful and continually give thanks to God; for this is the will for you in Christ Jesus.

1 Thessalonians 5:18 (AMP)

valley of despair and loss, it's required that I stay in God's presence longer to be filled; especially when we recognize God is our everything.

We often hear that worship is a form of prayer, so it is only right that the two go hand in hand during our seasons of loss. During and after our season of loss, it inspires so much intimacy with God. Because of that proximity and our new understanding of His character, it invariably requires our worship and adoration to rise. It makes us more receptive to God's wooing because we have experienced the presence of God. Who wouldn't serve a God like this? Truly to know God is to love Him and realize He is forever worthy of our praise, no matter the circumstance.

Wisdom & Understanding

This applies to us as well as to the word of God; we will undoubtedly come out of this season the wiser. The Bible tells us in Proverbs 4:7, "Wisdom is the principal thing; therefore get wisdom: And with all thy getting get understanding." Another translation

(NIV) says, "...though it cost you all you have..." as we reflect on what this season has cost us and tally it up with our spiritual eyes, it inspires a determination to make this season count and be "for something" and be the better for it. That could mean we're now searching the pages of scripture for knowledge which makes us wise already. Additionally, I've learned and am still learning quite a bit about processing hardship and transitions; even what I need from those in my life to support me. It's the wisdom of what I need and don't need that guides me in understanding what I need to navigate my loss, and hopefully is that way for you as well.

Thanksgiving

Whether we are in lack or in plenty, we recognize and become more thankful for what we had, what we have, and what we will gain. Thankful for the time we have had before it was gone, the privilege of knowing that person, the lessons, the journey– we lift our hands at the memory of it *all*.

Being thankful, even in the midst of loss, can be a hard thing to act out, but it is in this very thankfulness where God can intercede and remind us of 1 Thessalonians 5:18 AMP: "In every situation [no matter what the circumstances] be thankful and continually give thanks to God; for this is the will for you in Christ Jesus." This scripture admonishes us to be thankful no matter the circumstance and that to be thankful is a currency of sorts. We must adopt that posture of sitting in thankfulness as well as directing it back to God which pleases Him.

"When I survey the wondrous cross"

There is a beautiful Hymn by Issac Watts penned in 1701 titled, "When I survey the wondrous cross," [13] which captures the essence of the concept of realization of losses and gains I'd like to share:

When I survey the wondrous cross
on which the Prince of glory died,
my richest gain I count but loss,
and pour contempt on all my pride.

Forbid it, Lord, that I should boast
save in the death of Christ, my God!
All the vain things that charm me most,
I sacrifice them through his blood.

See, from his head, his hands, his feet,
sorrow and love flow mingled down.
Did e'er such love and sorrow meet,
or thorns compose so rich a crown?

Were the whole realm of nature mine,
that were a present far too small.
Love so amazing, so divine,
demands my soul, my life, my all.

This encapsulates the reflections and praise that are evoked when we think about the cross and Christ's sacrifice, as well as the pride we tie to what we esteem as "gain" before Christ's sacrifice gives our lives meaning and purpose, like Paul describes and we reviewed in Philippians chapter three. The only "thing" we can tie ourselves to is His sacrifice. In the fourth stanza, the world itself wouldn't be an adequate gift to put adjacent to Jesus. That last line (my favorite) gets me everytime: "love so amazing, so divine, demand my soul, my life, my all." My God! That love, that sacrifice just for *me*? That is more than worthy of my *all*. There is surely nothing that compares to that wondrous cross where my Savior–*our* Savior–bled and died. Jesus' love demanded the ultimate sacrifice of which we can never repay. Surely what He requires in this season of loss when we come into understanding that our life is His to will and blood brought down to our essence. In entirety, we are His and we willingly forfeit ourselves to our wondrous, loving Savior, Who is eternally worthy for the privilege. It is just that we may know Him. So friend, whatever it is, I implore you to willingly forfeit that thing at the foot of the cross for the gain that is Christ Jesus.

Key Points:

- God's Omniscience + God's subtraction = Purposeful Gain

- Even if we have nothing, we still have everything in Him (Phil. 3:7-10).

- Our lives are to be a reflection of Him and produce fruit on this earth (John 3:30).

Self Reflection & Exercise:

1. What subtraction has God made room for in your life? Identify three subtraction events God has used to make room in your life.

2. From the list of gains discussed in this chapter, select the gains you believe you are experiencing in your walk with Christ as a result of the subtraction.

3. Testify about how this gain has been purposeful to your life thus far.

4. What are some practical steps you can take to maintain a posture of Thankfulness?

5. Write a prayer to God thanking Him for these experiences and find a worship song/hymns that anchors you to this posture.

Notes

_____

_____

_____

_____

_____

_____

_____

_____

_____

Chapter 7

God Will Get the Glory from This

7

God Will Get the Glory from This

After all this this talk about losses, gains, and all that we've discussed, there's the question, the thought: will things get better? How will this season be beneficial? It's in no way my intention to spiritually bypass the very real feelings and emotions that this season has evoked because they're all valid; however, I am confident in encouraging us all that God will restore our hope, and He will also get glory from this season. Frankly, it's not necessarily one moment that occurs where we're suddenly over the loss, per se; it's more of an accumulation of moments that we find, stings less, that indicate we're nearing a healing pasture. This is where we can stand on the hills of peace and meet with the Lamb of God. For instance, the anniversary of the death, layoff, birthday, accident, life altering moment, is no longer a monument of despair but a marker of His faithfulness that has carried us since that time.

In the most surreal sense, it is almost like our hearts feel the periodic ache of missing that person, like an instinctual pang around that time and date when they left this earth. Although it has been years since they actually passed on or transitioned, it is amazing to think how much that initial pain has somehow abated and subsided. The adversary of our soul will lie to us and have us measure our subsided pain to the extent that we miss or had a relationship with who or what our lost to diminish the significance. It is a fallacy.

It's almost like, the further we get from that pain, the further or more distant the memory of that person becomes. If we truly had the distinct pleasure of knowing that loved one, the experience of knowing them, and had a viable relationship with them, then we can be assured we will always have affection for them. Some would say that if we do not feel it "like the day they left" then we must not miss them at all; however, that is far from scripture and reality. You mean to say that for the rest of my life we ought to feel immense sorrow and despair? By no means! Christ came to give life and life abundantly (John 10:10) and to give us a hope in Him.

It is then that we will indeed testify that God alone is the one who can revive hope to the heart once broken by circumstance. For those who mourn, God makes several promises us in Isaiah 61: 2-3 for us to cling to:

> To proclaim the acceptable year of the Lord, and
> the day of vengeance of our God; to comfort all
> that mourn; To appoint unto them that mourn in
> Zion, to give unto them beauty for ashes, the oil
> of joy for mourning, the garment of praise for the
> spirit of heaviness; that they might be called trees of
> righteousness, the planting of the Lord, that he might
> be glorified.

In the *Message* translation verse three reads, "Give them bouquets of roses instead of ashes, Messages of joy instead of news of doom, a praising heart instead of a languid spirit."

In all of these, they are contrary to what we may feel in the moment, yet the most assuring ones to hope in alongside his unrivaled comfort.

Grief and loss is not something we merely suffer through and are relegated to victimhood. When we go through it *with* God, it can be purposeful and we can be an active participant in our restoration with God. In Romans 11, Paul pens a beautiful doxology (hymn expressing praise and glory to God) for Israel in verses 33 through 36:

> Oh, the depth of the riches of the wisdom and
> knowledge of God! How unsearchable his judgments,
> and his paths beyond tracing out! Who has known the
> mind of the Lord? Or who has been his counselor?
> Who has ever given to God, that God should repay
> them? For from him and through him and for him are
> all things. To him be the glory forever! Amen.

A special notation to verse 36 from the Amplified version: "For from Him [all things originate] and through Him [all things live and exist] and to Him are all things [directed]." What this doxology signifies is that God is sovereign over His creation (i.e. you and I); therefore, everything originates from God, exists through God, and eventually serves His purpose. As we know from His sacrifice, it is a debt we can never repay nor is there anything we can give Him to bribe Him or extricate ourselves from the season in which we find ourselves; however, we can praise God knowing that He has a plan because praise is comely for the upright (Ps. 33:1).

There is yet hope

This season of loss is just that: a season on part of what is required in the crucible or especially tailored journey we are on being more like Him (also known as sanctification). God will often refine us through conditions that produce the best version ourselves, like refinement, to his satisfaction and that reflects Him. Reflecting God

But the fruit of the Spirit is love, joy, peace, longsuffering, kindness, goodness, faithfulness, gentleness, self-control. Against such there is no law.

Galatians 5:22-23

is how we bring Him glory. As such, He will refine us till He sees Himself, and as sovereign God, our permission is not required when He takes counsel with Himself. He factored in this piece for our ultimate gain and growth for reasons that go beyond now. I'm reminded of the *Westminster Shorter Catechism* which is a systematic Q&A approach to theological concepts. The first question asks, "What is the chief end of man?" The answer is, 'To glorify God and enjoy him forever' with reference to 1 Corinthians 10:31.[14] This is saying principally, in essence, whatever we do in this life with Christ, the purpose of our existence and time here is to *glorify* God– ergo, even our seasons (present included) will bring Him glory. Next to "enjoy him forever" denotes our reward, which is eternal life through Him.

For a moment, let's consider Jesus' example as our High priest in Hebrews 5:8b-9, as The Message translation says: "Because he honored God, God answered him. Though he was God's Son, he learned trusting-obedience by what he suffered, just as we do." Jesus is the Son of God and utterly blameless, yet He suffered.

If it pleased God to bruise His son, how much more are we, His creation, also at the disposition of His pleasure? He had to bruise His son because that was the redemptive means of saving us, but in that bruising was also the grace we otherwise would not have had, had He not bruised His only begotten son. It was in His grand redemptive, purposeful plan all along. So yes, we are hurt, yes we are crushed, but the God of *all* grace makes his strength perfect in our weakness and dispenses that to us in the midst of that (2 Cor. 12:9 MSG).

Whew! My God! What manner of love is this? Not comparable to any earthly person. Though this process is entirely personal, no one can go to the throne of grace for us; when we realize it is Him alone who delivers us from our despair, repairs our broken hearts, and restores it, that is worthy of our highest praise!

This level of crushing *must* produce fruit. So what does the restoration look like? It looks like the fruit of the spirit being produced, as it tells us in Galatians 5:22-23: "But the fruit of the Spirit is love, joy, peace, longsuffering, kindness, goodness, faithfulness, gentleness, self-control. Against such there is no law."

As much as we have a keen desire to replace what we lost and fill the void, God has the absolute ledger and is in charge of doing the restoring. Biblical restoration is a work of God– not human– to heal and renew us by bringing about positive changes in our lives. When we begin to see we have joy again after so many tears, love again when we thought we couldn't love anyone that much again, peace where we had unrest, and so on... our season has yielded that peaceable fruit the Father seeks (Heb. 12:11).

Truthfully, I had no inkling that my seasons of loss would produce this moment to come before you to encourage you (and encourage myself) now. I didn't see this day, nor did I see the fruit of it until I did. I didn't know I could endure long suffering until what I thought I wanted was no more. I didn't have gentleness or a burden for those grieving until I went through this. So I say this to encourage you, like I did myself, that there will be a time we both will look upon our season of loss with gratitude. We have to take solace knowing we will get through this season by God's grace, and in such a way, our Father in Heaven will get the glory. After all, that is our chief purpose in this life we still have the privilege to live. That is how He restores His own– by His hand and for His glory, in Jesus name.

Key Points:

- When we go through grief with God, it can be purposeful and we can be an active participant in our restoration with God.

- Crushing produces fruit so we can look more like Christ (Gal. 5:22-23).

- Restoration is a work of God, not man.

Self Reflection & Exercise:

1. What loss have you endured? Where in the midst of your healing did you give God glory?

2. In the midst of your season of loss, what scriptures have sustained you?

3. Looking at the fruits of the spirit (Gal. 5: 22-25) - which can you readily identify you have seen?

4. In what ways have you seen Him restore you? If not yet, how do you imagine you will feel as restored and whole?

5. Write a personal declaration for yourself: "I will be _____ [insert fruit] in this season." (Example: I will be **patient** in this season)

Notes

Chapter 8

Grief Is a Gateway

8

Grief is a Gateway

Our experience with grief and loss acts as a gateway to the throne of God whereby we receive His comfort, peace, and rest. A gate is an opening that is a means of entrance or exit to a protected city or structure. Typically you'll find a home, tower, city, etc. that the gate protects unauthorized guests from entering and must be unlocked to pass through. This presupposes that not just anyone can gain access and with conditions that you are permitted. Subsequently, the threshold or gateway must then be passed through upon entrance or exit. Frequently, people will drive by beautiful or even ominous gateways and don't stop; they only

This season is meant to inspire, praise, and adoration; and in doing so, God restores and heals our broken hearts.

pull into that driveway when they know the home or have a reason to access that property. Likewise, because life is seasonal, you may have seen people in your life or known of someone who experienced the kinds of losses we've discussed, but it never quite hit home for you. Truthfully, we know that this was not ideally where you'd stop, but now you have cause to access the property (throne) because you need to gain access (to God).

When I reflect on my own life (and have done quite a bit of it in these pages), I remember hearing about people who lost loved ones while I was in grade school and extended my condolences without full experiential reference until it was my season to walk through it. As a child, both my grandfathers passed, but I didn't quite grasp the concept until I was in my adulthood, where I went through what felt like consecutive seasons of loss– from my physical faculties after traumatic injuries to loved ones who were passing away annually in a five-year span.

Psalm 100 tells us in verse 4 that we should, "Enter into his gates with thanksgiving, and into his courts with praise: be thankful unto him, and bless his name." The Message translation says, "Enter with the password: 'Thank you!' Make yourselves at home, talking praise. Thank him. Worship him." Like so, grief and loss presents us with a unique opportunity to access God on the condition of thanksgiving, in

We must enter without trepidation but with confidence, knowing we are fully seen, known, carried, and loved by God.

order to meet God afresh. This season is meant to inspire, praise, and adoration; and in doing so, God restores and heals our broken hearts. We will find there is much to yet thank God for.

As a gateway is meant to be passed through, the gate will also keep us enclosed *safely* in the courts of our God, at His throne, in His loving arms. Don't pass through for the sake of traversing, nor dwell on the outside of the threshold in pain, but dwell *in* the loss that brought us to the gateway where we can meet God so that when we exit, we will leave newly transformed and restored because we received His comfort, peace, and rest.

We ought to let grief be the gateway to His throne of grace and take our cue from Hebrews 4:16 where we are encouraged to do the following: "Let us then approach God's throne of grace with confidence, so that we may receive mercy and find grace to help us in our time of need."

It is an act of faith to stand at the threshold, grief in hand, but friend, you and I have come so far already. That's why Paul admonishes us Hebrews 11:6 with this: "He who comes to God must believe that He is, and that He is a rewarder of those who diligently seek Him." We have been brought to this point by circumstance, and yet are believing in the God of our salvation and determined to seek Him out in our grief. Because when we seek Him, we will find Him when we seek Him with our whole heart (Jeremiah 29:13). So, Christ is the reward on the other side of the gate, should we decide not to let our trials separate us from Him. We must enter without trepidation but with confidence, knowing we are fully seen, known, carried, and loved by God. It is because we know in whom we believe and who is waiting for us. Friend, resist not His wooing; this loss, this season, and this experience is intentionally crafted to draw each of us back to the arms of our heavenly Father. We will not be overtaken except by His unfailing love when we agree to pass through the gates of grief.

Finally, we have to ask: what is grief a gateway to? As much as grief can be an isolated experience, it is often the gateway to richer, undeniable encounters and experiences we wouldn't experience the same such as an encounter with His character. By accessing the facets of His character, we get to learn of God intimately and experientially because we are invited to experience who He is. The names of God become our favorite contact list. He becomes Jehovah Raah (the Lord my shepard), Jehovah Shalom (the Lord our peace), Jehovah Rapha (the Lord who heals), Jehovah Shammah (the Lord who is there) and so much more.

There, in the understanding of God and His character, we will find our purpose. We won't leave this world empty because we felt deeply, and allowing this season to produce in us was part of our course and unique journey, not wanting to leave this world empty. We sometimes wonder how loss can equate to gain. It may feel as though that is the last "benefit" in this season, but we will gain access to another facet of the character of God when we enter with thanksgiving to pass through the gate to grieve *with* Him. Be assured we will walk out restored.

In closing, I am reminded of the hymn, "Because He lives" by Bill & Gloria Gaither (1971). The chorus says:

> *Because He lives, I can face tomorrow,*
> *Because He lives, all fear is gone;*
>
> *Because I know He holds the future,*
> *And life is worth the living,*
> *Just because He lives!*

Be encouraged, my friend. He lives and so shall we; there is yet more life to live after this season. Rest assured, God will restore and get the glory from this season of our lives. Grief is not to preclude us from entering the gateway; it is actually an invitation to our depleted souls by which we can enter freely to receive His comfort, rest, and restoration with full assurance that when we transition into the next season, we will do so fuller than when we came.

Key Points:

- Our experience with grief and loss acts as a gateway to the throne of God whereby we receive His comfort, peace, and rest.

- Grief is the gateway to richer, undeniable encounters with His Character.

- Thanksgiving is the password at the gate to safely grieve with Him in His courts, at His throne, in His loving arms.

Self Reflection & Exercise:

1. How have you allowed grief to be a barrier instead of a gateway to the throne of God?

2. In what ways do you see grief differently now?

3. List the names of God that accompany the character you need Him to show up as in your life. (Example: *Jehovah Shalom*, The Lord is Peace, I need you to be my peace today.)

Notes

_____

_____

_____

_____

_____

_____

_____

_____

_____

_____

Conclusion

Loss, as we know it, is an absence– whether it is removed or deprived– that leaves a void. The things or people we lose do not have to be the end of us but the beginning, a chance to appreciate the growth that waits on the other side, because loss is not a closed door. It is not just a natural experience; it is spiritual. Loss is the door– the experience of grief acts as the gateway. While we grieve, it becomes a path that God has created to invite us in to greet Him and to be embraced in His loving arms.

We ought not to interpret our losses– that death, that relationship ending, that failed promotion, that totaled car– as barriers to God, even though our broken hearts tell us that it is, because grief is not (nor does it have to be) a grave– it's a gateway. When we pass through the gate, we get to fix our eyes on Him and who He is to us. The beauty of grief in this season is that God does not leave us in our loss; He gives us hope during it because *He* is our hope by giving us Himself.

Ultimately, God wants to usher us into a place of healing, to transform us. In all that we lose, God, through Jesus Christ, wants us to gain so much more than the tangible and material things of this world. They are temporary because they can be taken at any time. In going through our own tailored gateways of grief after our loss, we are being shaped and molded into who God is calling us to be. That way, when we emerge, we will emerge on the other side of that gateway, stronger and with more gain than the loss that brought us to the season. Therefore, we can fix our eyes on Him, knowing who He is in that experience: hope. Our hope in Him is what makes grief sacred and allows us to put our hope in Christ with confidence because God doesn't leave us in our loss; He gives us hope in it.

And finally, when we stand at the gateway of grief, we are confronted with God, as well as ourselves, with the hopes of safely passing through to both encounter and receive His peace, rest, and comfort. Gateways are meant to be passages, and thanksgiving is the password that grants us access to safely grieve with Him. We are able to access God and His many characteristics that make Him who He is to and for us.

So, my friend, I pray you have been encouraged to accept the invitation to enter through the sacred gateway, wherein a special encounter with your Father awaits, Who longs to meet you with His arms of comfort. Now, the next time grief is at your door, it is my hope that you will view it differently by remembering the **G.A.T.E.W.A.Y.**:

Give your losses to God by counting your gains in Him (Philippians 3:7-10).

Acknowledge the loss(es) in this season (2 Corinthians 4:8-9).

Thanksgiving by giving thanks to God and use it as your password at the gate (Psalm 100:4).

Examine your heart and what that loss means to you (Psalm 139:23-24).

Worship God even when it hurts because He is the Lord and a great God (Psalm 95).

Agree with God's decision (Psalm 119:67-68).

Yield your Heart to God and to the journey of grief so you can receive His peace & comfort (Philippians 4:7).

Endnotes

1. Wright, H. N. (2011). The complete guide to crisis & trauma counseling: What to Do and Say When It Matters Most! Gospel Light Publications.

2. Swaggart, J. (2006). The expositor's study Bible: Giant Print Edition.

3. Stevenson, J.W. (2010) "Our Eyes Are Still On You." *Nation of Praise*. Heirs Publishing Company.

4. Jacobs, H. (5 May, 2003). Comfort - International Standard Bible Encyclopaedia. Retrieved from https://www.blueletterbible.org/search/Dictionary/viewTopic.cfm

5. G3870 - parakaleō - Strong's Greek Lexicon (kjv). Retrieved from https://www.blueletterbible.org/lexicon/g3870/kjv/tr/0-1/

6. G3875 - paraklētos - Strong's Greek Lexicon (kjv). Retrieved from https://www.blueletterbible.org/lexicon/g3875/kjv/tr/0-1/

7. G3107 - makarios - Strong's Greek Lexicon (kjv). Retrieved from https://www.blueletterbible.org/lexicon/g3107/kjv/tr/0-1/

8. H3615 - kālâ - Strong's Hebrew Lexicon (kjv). Retrieved from https://www.blueletterbible.org/lexicon/h3615/kjv/wlc/0-1/

9. G2771 - kerdos - Strong's Greek Lexicon (kjv). Retrieved from https://www.blueletterbible.org/lexicon/g2771/kjv/tr/0-1/

10. G2233 - hēgeomai - Strong's Greek Lexicon (kjv). Retrieved from https://www.blueletterbible.org/lexicon/g2233/kjv/tr/0-1/

11. G2209 - zēmia - Strong's Greek Lexicon (kjv). Retrieved from https://www.blueletterbible.org/lexicon/g2209/kjv/tr/ss0/0-1

12. Watts, I. "When I survey the wondrous cross" (1701). Hymnary. org. https://hymnary.org/text/when_i_survey_the_wondrous_cross_watts

13. Williamson, G. I. (2003). *The Westminster Shorter Catechism: For Study Classes*. P & R Publishing.

14. Wyse, E. (2006). *The Christian Life Hymnal*. Hendrickson Publishers.

About the Author

Guerlyne Guercy is a writer, speaker, and encourager, born and raised in New York and currently resides in Texas. She holds a bachelors in Psychology and an MBA. She now uses her talents and calling to meet people in the tender places of their grief with hope rooted in Jesus. Guerlyne's expressed hope is to help others see loss not as the end, but as an invitation into deeper intimacy with God. *Grief Is a Gateway* is her debut book.

CONTACT

You can follow Guerlyne on Facebook and Instagram **@GuerlyneG.**

If you would like to have Guerlyne speak at your event you can find more information at **www.GuerlyneGuercy.com.**